DSE (MR)
MANUAL

Utilization and Maintenance of Teaching-Learning Material (TLM)

DSE (MR)
MANUAL

Utilization and Maintenance of Teaching-Learning Material (TLM)

Smt. Suman Sindhu

Edited by:

Prof. P. Jayachandran
Dr. Sumit Roy

Rehabilitation Council of India
in association with

KANISHKA PUBLISHERS, DISTRIBUTORS
NEW DELHI-110 002

KANISHKA PUBLISHERS, DISTRIBUTORS
4697/5-21A, Ansari Road, Daryaganj
New Delhi -110 002
Phones : 2327 0497, 2328 8285
Fax : 011-2328 8285
E-mail : kanishka_publishing@yahoo.co.in
kanishkabooks@gmail.com

Utilization and Maintenance of Teaching-Learning Material (TLM)
Edition-2023

PRINTED IN INDIA

Published by Madan Sachdeva for Kanishka Publishers, Distributors, 4697/5-21A, Ansari Road, Daryaganj, New Delhi-110002, Typeset by Sunshine Graphics, Delhi, and Printed at G.S. Printers, Delhi.

Foreword

"A book that fills the mind with beauty and opens the heart to what is lovely and lovable is a treasure forever". It allows transmission of knowledge from generation to generation and from place to place. Books have always been our best friend and a source of learning. We read and write for many purposes, most of the time they are either social or academic.

This manual attempts to serve the academic needs in the field of Special Education and Rehabilitation. Disability Studies are mostly dependent on western books and literature with very little being available within the country. An effort has been made to fill in the gaps that existed, by preparing the manuals that would be simple in approach, easy to understand and serving the students needs. We hope that they will prove to be an effective tool not only for students and teachers, but also for parents, NGOs and organizations of persons with disability. The manual attempts to consciously follow the course syllabus and in the process explore the general and disability specific issues. In the process of creating such specifically tailored manuals for the courses, there are possibilities of oversights or errors despite our being careful. The Council would like to invite your suggestions and comments so that the subsequent editions, revised versions can be improved upon.

Time and again, it was emphasized that there is a great dearth of study material for the students as well as the teachers for the various diploma level courses in discipline of Special Education and Rehabilitation of the Council. This set the Council to take up the onerous task of manual preparation. Lots of effort has gone into the process, by the authors and the editors. Searching for the appropriate and relevant material that should go into the manual, readily understood by the trainee has been a gigantic responsibility executed with extreme care by the specialist team chosen for this purpose.

The Council would like to thank everyone associated with this project for their contribution. We hope that the manuals are able to unlock the doors of knowledge and successfully develop an insight into the world of persons with disability.

(Dr. J.P. Singh)
Member-Secretary

Contents

Introduction

The Indian National Education Policy in 1964-65 outlined the importance of teaching aids in these words. "The supply of teaching aids to every school is essential for the improvement of the quality of teaching. It would indeed bring about an educational revolution in the country." In 1986, the National Policy on Education (NPE) also instituted "Operation Blackboard" scheme for schools. Wherein, every school was to be provided by the State Governments with a good blackboard and modern teaching materials and aids including a radio and a tape recorder.

Thus, it is a recognized fact by the experts that teaching aids and teaching materials are very helpful in teaching- learning process, both for the normal and children with Mental Retardation (M.R.). In fact, their utility is much more manifest in the case of children with mental retardation because their intellectual functioning is sub-average and may also be suffering form many other disabilities such as visual and hearing impairments and speech defects. Therefore, Special educators/Teachers must know the value of teaching materials and teaching aids for both individual and group teaching programmes for children with mental retardation. They should never fully rely on verbal teaching because it is least effective with such children. They should use visual aids and also provide practical learning experiences to the children in real life situations. Thus, a good special teacher is that who uses less verbal methods, but more activity methods of teaching and learning for these children.

OBJECTIVES

On completion of this topic the trainee is expected to exhibit competency in:

1. Selection and preparation of TLM and need specific aids.
2. Using appropriate technologies in Teaching-Learning Materials and functional aids.

UNIT–1

STRUCTURE

- Identifying the Need for Use of TLM
- Importance of Teaching Aids
- Research on Left and Right Brain Functioning
- Other Researches on Senses
- Edgar Dale's Cone of Learning Experiences
- Developing Needs Specified Aid
- Age Appropriate Material
- Aid for Teaching Functional Skills
- Making of Teaching Aids
- Role of Special Educators in Making Teaching Aids
- Unit Summary
- Check Your Progress
- Assignment/Activities
- Point for Discussion/Clarification

Unit–1

Identifying the Need for Use of TLM

It is widely accepted fact that activity based or active participation method of teaching provides the best learning experience to all the children with or without disability. Where the teacher opts for the easiest method of teaching through verbal mode only, students also forgets easily. Adding visual aids like picture, chart, diagrams, model etc., added beauty and easy learning for the students. However, verbal, visual and activity combined together is the best method of teaching with person with mental retardation.

Importance of Teaching Aids

There is a popular saying about teaching and learning, which a special teacher should note:

What I hear, I forget
What I see, I remember
What I do, I know

Or

A Visual Conveys More Than
Ten Thousand Words Can Do

Significance and Value of Teaching Materials and Aids is Indicated by These Benefits:

1. Children are easily motivated for learning with the help of teaching materials and aids.

2. With them, they actively participate in teaching learning process in the classroom.
3. Teacher can handle the task of teaching more effectively with the help of such aids.
4. Children get excited and enthused due to meaningful learning with illustrations and aids.
5. Children respond well to the stimuli provided by such aids and retain as well as remember lessons, over a longer period.
6. Children get fully interested and involved in manipulating such aids and there by develop many skills such as motor skills. Communication skills, cognitive skills and prevocational skills.
7. Abstract ideas and concepts are clearly concretized through pictures and models and children enjoy learning those concepts.
8. Large groups can be handled by teacher easily with the help of such materials in the class.
9. Teacher in class also saves time and energy due to the fact that pictures describe and depict the ideas more distinctly and quickly.
10. Psychological researches indicate that teaching materials and aids promote multi sensory learning, which is needed for children with M.R.

Research on Left and Right Brain Functioning

Researches on the functioning of left and right brain (Gilder, 1985 and Edgeron, 1989) have convinced that visuals are most effective to assimilate information because these activate both the right and left parts of brain as compared to the verbal which activates only the left side brain.

The diagram below shows the place of variety of content in left and Right Brain (Next Page).

Other Researches on Senses

A large number of research evidence is available on the effectiveness of various senses in relation to learning. The pie diagram given below depicts the role or effectiveness of various senses in learning.

It is clear from the above research evidences that of all the five senses sight, hearing, touch small and taste, visual part contributes

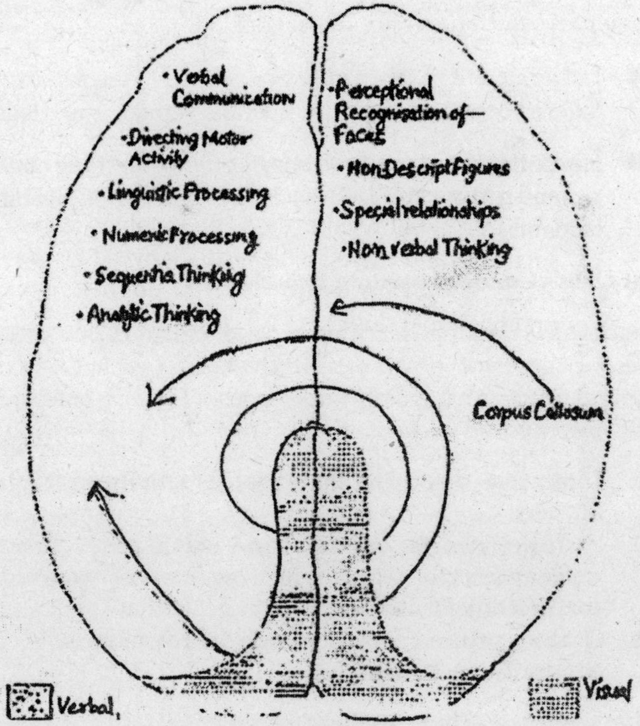

Left and Right

Figure 1: Left and Right Brain

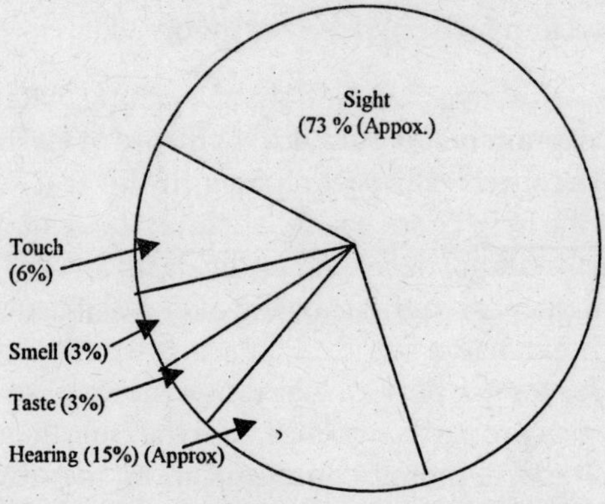

Figure 2: Pie Diagram

the maximum, which is nearly 73 per cent in learning, whereas the hearing part contributes only 15 per cent.

- Learning will be more effective and up-to the maximum, if different senses, particularly visual and verbal are used together.
- Hence the use of multi-sensory teaching-learning materials increases the effectiveness of the process of learning in students.

Edgar Dale's Cone of Learning Experiences

Edgar dale has classified learning experiences into Cone known as 'Cone of Experience' based on effectiveness of each. Cone of the learning experience has mainly three stages of learning or techniques of teaching children in class.

1. Direct sensory contact that involves activity on the part of learners.
2. Pictures charts, models and such other forms of representation of objects, which involve observation, on the part of learners.
3. Oral or printed words which involve symbols, to be interpreted by the learners.

Hence, it is clear how teaching material and teaching aids of all kinds such as visual, audio-visual and activity aids are very essential for special teacher in day-to-day work.

The best source of learning is the direct "motor-sensory" or activity method in which children are involved.

It is clear from above that the help of teaching material and aids for learning easily motivates all children. By use of teaching material and aids children actively participates in the teaching-learning process. With the help of such aids teaching the students becomes more effective. Excitation level and enthusiasm level of the students are very high with meaningful learning aids and illustration. Lesson learnt through extensive use of aids are remembered easily and remembered for longer period. With high motivation and interest level children gets properly involved with the aids; they manipulate the aids, which add to motor, communication, cognitive and other skills. Children find it difficult to learn or acquire abstract ideas, the

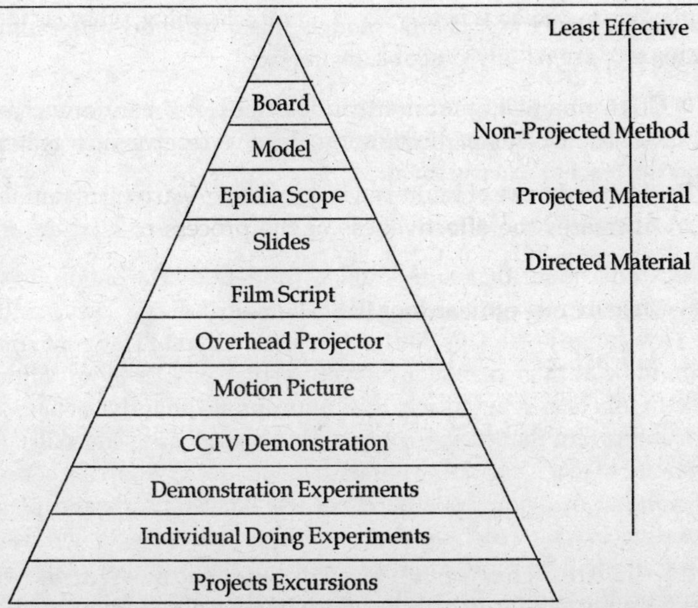

Figure 3 : Dale's Cone of Experiences

concrete material and aids makes the learning enjoyable. Group of children can be easily managed by planned teaching aids. Teacher saves lot of time and energy in the class, as most of the aids are powerful enough themselves to teach the concept.

Developing Need Specified Aid

Different groups of person have different roles, motives and in preparing aids for person with mental retardation.

For a particular class and the students of the class, the teacher is the best judge to decide the best aid. These aids made by the teacher with the help of other teacher, senior students etc., may not be very well furnished but these aids serve the basic purpose of teaching-learning in classroom. Professional experts can well explain and illustrate some technical concepts and complex task by making charts, tables, models, graphs etc. These aids are expensive and most school cannot afford such aids.

Many educational aids are manufactured in large scale by companies Science kit, geometry kit, films, audio, video, slides, software, hardware, charts, models, historical and geographical maps etc., are widely available in market.

Government department publish posters, banners, charts, graphs etc., for public distribution. Schools receive such material and the teacher can use them.

Age Appropriate Material

It is well-known that individual with mental retardation do not have their mental age matching their chronological age. They function at a lower age level. This does not mean that the skill taught to them should be at their mental age level. As one expects these children also to function in the society with appropriate adaptive behaviour, it is important that they are exposed to age-appropriate skills. For instance to teach an adolescent with mental retardation the concept of number or colour, one need not use blocks, beads and plastic building bricks. Teaching these concepts with objects one use in daily life will be more appropriate. Counting number plates and cups on the dining table while getting the person to arrange the table or talking of the colour of vegetables like tomato, beans and so on while buying or storing them will be more age appropriate. It would also lead to learning domestic skills in addition to colour and number. One should involve the children with mental retardation in the activities of daily routine and use the opportunities for incidental teaching with the materials in the home.

Aid for Teaching Functional Skills

Children with mental retardation have limited capacity to learn and therefore, whatever is taught must be functional oriented, leading to words independence in day-to-day life. The learning or educational aid used should be as far as possible, materials that the child will have to use in his daily life, rather than on simulated. This provides an opportunity for the child to learn the skill directly. For instance, if the child has to be taught fixing buckles the best way to teach is by using his own belt or buckle rather than those on wooden frames.

Making of Teaching Aids

Different agents with different motives and varied skills make teaching aids for children with mental retardation. Their role is briefly described here as under.

Teachers

They are the best judges to decide. What kinds of aids are needed for children in their classes? Some of them can easily make them by themselves or with the help of students in the school. Such aids may not be perfectly furnished. Yet they serve the purpose of teaching-learning in classroom.

Professional Experts

Some technical concepts and complex ideas can be well illustrated by them in the form of charts, models, tables, graphs and so on. Such aids are likely to be expensive and many schools may not be able to afford to buy them for teachers and students.

Commercial Companies

There are many commercial companies, which specialize in manufacturing education materials and teaching aids for school children. They can supply historical and geographic maps, scientific kits, mathematical instruments, films and filmstrips, audio and visual hardware.

Government Agencies

Every State Government has a statistical bureau and publicity department, which produce annual reports, figures and facts in the form of charts and pictures for free public distribution. They send such materials to schools also, so that teachers and students use in classroom instruction on various subjects.

Role of Special Educators in Making Teaching Aids

The teacher must be observant, keen, motivated, creative and have scientific and artistic temperament to make teaching aids and make it a habit or a regular affair of teaching-learning programmer. He may do the following things.

1. Waste and used material of the class, school, teacher's home, student's home etc., can be effectively used for making various teaching aids.
2. The children of the class may themselves be motivated and involved in search of waste material and preparation of aids.
3. Planning and preparing of teaching aids not only helps in

the learning the concept but also add to development of fine motor, eye hand coordination, prevocational, communication and cognitive skill.

4. The person with mental retardation shall be motivated, develop confidence and have feeling of well-being by involving themselves in such activities.

Unit Summary

After going through the above unit, it may be concluded that Special Educators should select the appropriate teaching material in teaching the person with mental retardation. To make the teaching more effective the teacher should select Kinesthetic Approach with other senses. This method of combining verbal, visual and other activities together help the teacher to motivate the children easily, their active participation in teaching-learning process more effectively, saves time and energy etc., the teacher should develop specific aid based on the need of the child with mental retardation. TLM should be the age appropriate and functional utility usually used in his daily life because the children with M.R. have limited capacity. These TLM may be prepared by the special educators by using the waste and used materials. Some technical TLM like charts, models, labels, graphs—prepared by professional experts, commercial companies and government agencies may be used. The use of effective, age appropriate, functional and need based TLM help in developing confidence by involving the children with M.R. in such activities. Thus, Special Educators may play a key role in this activity.

Check Your Progress

1. "Teaching Aid and Teaching Material are very helpful in teaching-learning process." Discuss.
2. What do you mean by Edgar Dale's cone of learning experience? Explain it with diagram.
3. What is the role of Special Educator in preparing TLM?
4. What are the benefits of TLM in teaching the children with mental retardation?
5. What is Pie Diagram?
6. Define low cost teaching aids.
7. How do you select appropriate teaching methods and aids?

8. Write the importance of age appropriate teaching-learning material?
9. Explain TLM.
10. What is functional oriented TLM? Give any two examples.

Assignment/Activities

What is the importance of teaching Aids? Prepare two low cost teaching aids for each category (mild, moderate and severe mentally retarded children) of primary group by using eye-hand co-ordination.

Point for Discussion/Clarification

After going through the unit trainees may like to have further discussion on some points and clarification on other. They may note down these points for further discussion.

UNIT–2

STRUCTURE

- Concept of Learning Aids and Functional Aids
- Difference between Teaching Material and Teaching Aid
- The Teaching Aids and the Functional Aids
- Defining Multi-Sensory Teaching-Learning Material
- Multi-Sensory Teaching-Learning Materials and Audio-Visual Aids
- Effectiveness of Multi-Sensory Teaching-Learning Materials: What Researches Say?
- Effective Use of Multi-Sensory Teaching-Learning Material
- Selection of Multi-Sensory Teaching-Learning Materials
- Unit Summary
- Check Your Progress
- Assignment/Activities
- Point for Discussion/Clarification

Unit–2

Concept of Learning Aids and Functional Aids

As stated earlier the teaching aid and teaching material are very helpful in teaching-learning process for person with disability like normal children. The use and utility of these aid is in fact far more and wide with person with disability. Person with mental retardation is very much dependent on effective teaching-learning aid to learn skill. Because of low intellectual functioning, associated conditioning, sensory impairment and speech defect, the use of teaching learning aid is very important and indispensable.

As out line in the Indian National Education Policy of 1964-66, "The supply of teaching aid to every school is essential for the improvement of quality of teaching. It would bring about an educational revolution in the country." The National Policy of Education (NPE, 1986) instituted "operation blackboard scheme for school, where in every school was to be provided by the State Government with a good blackboard and modern teaching material and aid, including a radio and a tape recorder."

All special educators must regard the extensive use of teaching material and teaching aid for working with person with mental retardation in both individual and group setting, relying on blackboard or on verbal teaching alone is less effective and not suggested. Tactile, visual, auditory, kinesthetic, practical learning experience and real life situation are suggested method to help person with mental retardation learning faster and better. For best learning a good teacher shall use less verbal method and more visual and concrete level experience in teaching their children.

Difference between Teaching Material and Teaching Aid

Teaching aid is a smaller and narrower term than teaching material or instructional material. In degree of application both are widely different but in kind they appear similar.

Teaching material can be widely used as textbook, handbook, lesson notes, lecture notes, programmes, references or sources material etc. For use of students and teacher teaching these students; the teaching material are prepared by high level of experts or professional in their field of specialization. The teaching material covers the topics as per course or syllabus to be covered by the students and teachers. Planning implementation and evaluation of the students are done with the help of these materials. They are very popular for self-study under open learning, distance learning and E-learning programme. Regular students are also helped through self-study of these materials.

On the other hand, charts, pictures, models, graphs, video, audio, filmstrips, slides, transparent sheets, concrete objects etc., are called teaching aids. These materials can be prepared by the teacher of the respective classes, other trained teachers, experts or even by commercial agencies. In academic and non-academic activities, these teaching aids are aids to the teacher, student and teaching-learning process in dealing with individual or a particular group helps in teaching strategies. Students get motivation, attend to the activity and learn easily by the use of these aids. The teacher also saves time in classroom by effective use of teaching aids.

The Teaching Aids and the Functional Aids

When a teaching aid is used for learning a concept it is technically referred to as teaching aids. Once a concept is learnt the utility of the specific learning aid is reduced. Like a picture album to teach a name of common objects is used as a learning aid in a classroom. Once a student learns the names of the objects; the use of the album reduces and gradually totally faded.

In functional aids students keep using the teaching aids even after learning the concepts. In case of children with no speech, the photo album is continued to be used as communication tool; this refers to functional aids. Special educator often uses both learning aids and functional aids during classroom teaching.

With the person with mental retardation multi sensory learning is recommended. Research clearly indicates use of teaching aids enhances the multi-sensory input to the children.

10.0 per cent through taste
1.5 per cent through touch
3.5 per cent through smell
11.0 per cent through hearing
83.0 per cent through sight
And we remember
20 per cent of what we hear
30 per cent of what we see
50 per cent of what we see and hear
80 per cent of what we see, hear and do

The above paragraph gives a clear view of how teaching material and teaching aids of different kinds such as tactile, auditory, visual, audio-visual and activity aids are very essential for teachers and students for regular teaching-learning process. The best method however is the method of using "sensory motor" and activity method.

Defining Multi-Sensory Teaching-Learning Material

You might have heard about this term from your school days. Your teachers also might have used some of these multi-sensory teaching-learning material in the classroom or in other teaching-learning situations. But when I ask what does multi-sensory teaching-learning material mean, then many of you may not be able to answer it properly and accurately. Different people might give answers, which will vary from one-another. Let us find out what does multi-sensory teaching-learning material means to you?

You might have defined multi-sensory teaching-learning materials as one of the following or something very similar:

- Teaching-learning material related to sense
- A variety of teaching-learning material.

- A teaching-learning material, which improves the effectiveness of learning.

Your attempt to define multi-sensory teaching-learning material is in the right direction. Multi-sensory teaching-learning material means partially all these and many more.

We may also define multi-sensory teaching-learning material as:

- A kind of teaching-learning material, which helps a student in acquiring appropriate learning experience using the sense organs, related to vision, hearing, touch, smell and taste.
- Aids to teaching and learning which utilizes several senses.

Multi-Sensory Teaching-Learning Materials and Audio-Visual Aids

Multi-sensory teaching-learning materials are different from the traditional activities of the school such as reading and writing. In fact, audio-visual teaching-learning materials are multi-sensory in nature. When using multi-sensory teaching-learning materials, the students are experiencing something different. For example, variety is always attractive to a student. In multi-sensory teaching-learning materials, focus is always on the use of variety of sense organs, which are out gateways of acquiring learning experiences; Multi-sensory teaching-learning materials being sensory materials captivate attention, which is so intense that other things are excluded from a person's mind. It is very rightly said that:

What I hear, I forget.
What I see, I remember.
What I do, I know.

Or

A Visual Conveys More Than what
Ten Thousands Words Can Do

Effectiveness of Multi-Sensory Teaching-Learning Materials: What Researches Say?

With the development of the utility of multi-sensory teaching-learning material in maximizing the effectiveness of learning, a number of researchers all over the world initiated researches in order to find out the effectiveness of multi-senses in the teaching-learning process. Some of the research findings and then interpretations are given in the Unit 1 as Dale's Cone of Experience, pie diagram and researches on Left and Right Brain Functioning.

The relative effectiveness of these experiences is illustrated by Dale as a 'Cone of Experience' with verbal talk at the apex level being least effective and project excursions proving direct experience at the base of the cone as most effective. The experience provided through multi-senses is given only when it is not possible to give direct experience.

Researches on the functioning of left and right brain (Gilder, 1985 and Edgeron, 1989) have convinced even the severest critics of the use of technology as instructional material for learning. Visuals are most effective to assimilate information because these activate both the right and left parts of the brain as compared to the verbal, which activates only the left side brain.

Research evidences on the effectiveness of various senses in learning shows that of all the five senses namely: sight, hearing, touch, smell and taste the visual part contributes the maximum which is nearly 73 per cent in learning, whereas the hearing part contributes only around 15 per cent. Learning will be more effective and up-to the maximum, if different senses, particularly visual and verbal, are used together.

On the basis of all the above research evidences, it can be very well inferred that use of multi-sensory teaching-learning materials increases the effectiveness of the process of learning in students.

Effective Use of Multi-Sensory Teaching-Learning Material

In the changing scenario of teaching teachers have a large number of multi-sensory materials to use in the classroom and also outside the classroom to create an environment for learning.

While using these multi-sensory materials for teaching-learning, teachers may consider the following points:

1. The teacher must know the specific function of the teaching-learning material.
2. Material must be used at the proper place in the lesson at the beginning, in the middle, at the end depending upon its use.

3. The teacher must know how to use the various materials effectively.
4. The material selected for use should be appropriate to the age, intelligence and experience of the students.
5. There should be student's participation in the material.
6. The teacher should use the material with pre-and post-discussion sessions.
7. Those who use them should continuously evaluate the material.

Selection of Multi-Sensory Teaching-Learning Materials

The relative effectiveness of different types of teaching-learning materials in different situations depends on their classification and selection. Most of the teaching-learning materials can perform many instructional functions to some extent but others are better at doing certain things, with no single material being best for all purposes. It is very important to workout the situations in which these materials are most effective. This will make it possible to foresee the part, which a particular material can play, and to prepare a well-balanced use. Selection and choice of teaching-learning material depends upon a variety of factors such as the following:

1. Nature of learning task, that is, facts, concepts, principles and skills etc.
2. Mode of teaching-learning, that is whether in classroom or out of classroom, in large group or in small group.
3. Student characteristics like entry-level behaviour and level of knowledge.
4. Cost and technology resources available.

Besides the above, the choice of suitable material also depends on some of the practical factors such as the range of viewing and hearing distance for the use of multi-sensory material, ease of handling or interrupting material to permit student response and provide feedback and teacher competence required for operating the material.

Unit Summary

From this unit we may sum up that learning aids are used for leaning a concept which has utility to learn specific skills/concepts. As the concept acquired and gradually learnt, the learning aids are also gradually faded out. While the functional aids are used even after learning the concepts because these aids are commonly used in the immediate environment of children with mental retardation and have great utility in day-to-day life to become independent. At the initial stage both learning aids and functional aids are used side by side but learning aids are gradually faded fully. These learning aids and functional aids both enhance the multi-sensory input of the children. In such a way we are using multi-sensory teaching-learning material which means extensive use of several senses to improve the effectiveness of learning. All the audio-visual aids are included in multi-sensory teaching-learning aids which develop the utility and effectiveness of learning. These aids should be selected and used very carefully and effectively so that the children with mental retardation can learn effectively with more experiences. Here the co-operation between teacher and parents and knowledge of environment at home are very essential for selection of the functional aids.

Check Your Progress

1. Discuss the role of functional aids and learning aids in teaching children with special needs.
2. What are the concepts of learning aids and functional aids? Write the difference between these two.
3. Explain in brief the effectiveness of multi-sensory teaching-learning materials.
4. How do you use effectively the multi-sensory teaching-learning material?
5. How do you select the multi-sensory teaching-learning material for the children with special needs?
6. Define multi-sensory learning aids.
7. Explain VAKT.
8. Give two examples of teaching material.
9. Give two examples of teaching aids.
10. Give two examples of functional aids.

Assignment/Activities

Define multi-sensory teaching-learning material. Prepare five multi-sensory teaching-learning material which help a student with special needs in acquiring appropriate learning experiences by using any sense organ related to vision, hearing, touch, smell and taste for the children with mental retardation in the age group of 14 years.

Point for Discussion/Clarification

After going through the unit trainees may like to have further discussion on some points and clarification on other. They may note down these points for further discussion.

UNIT–3

STRUCTURE

- Adaptive/Assistive Devices for Children with Associated Disabilities – CP, Autism and Multiple Disabilities
- Use of Assistive Devices
- Acquisitional of Self-Care Skills
- Children with Mental Retardation with Motor Problems in General Classroom
- Guidelines for Teaching Motor Skills
- Meeting Educational Needs
- Positioning the Child in Class
- School Responsibilities
- Teacher's Role
- Some Examples of Assistive Devices
- Unit Summary
- Check Your Progress
- Assignment/Activities
- Point for Discussion/Clarification

Unit–3

Adaptive/Assistive Devices for Children with Associated Disabilities—CP, Autism and Multiple Disabilities

Delay in motor development occurs because of persistence of primitive reflexes and delay in the attainment of the automatic ones. Three elements (which are tone, control and strength) are basic building blocks for all motor activities. It is the abnormality in these three elements that underlies motor problem seen in children with associated disabilities. Treatment procedure including (physiotherapy and occupational therapy) can help the child attain automatic reflexes. Sometimes adaptive devices are used to help the child function as independently as possible.

Adaptive devices are specially designed devices and custom modifications may be necessary to enable driving power steering, power brakers and automatic transmission may be adequate adaptations for the less severely disabled person. Along with adaptive devices, activities are also planned to facilitate the child to learn skills and functions in which he is lacking.

Use of Assistive Devices

Along with physiotherapy in certain cases, depending on the need, aids and assistive devices are employed to help children function as independently as possible. The child who is unable to learn to walk freely may be helped to use.

1. Walker

2. Crutches
3. Cane
4. Wheelchair.

Use of Walkers

There are several types of walkers as illustrated below. The infant walker is designed for children from 1½ to 4 years of age. The child walker is for children from 2 to 8 years who are not expected to be ambulatory in future.

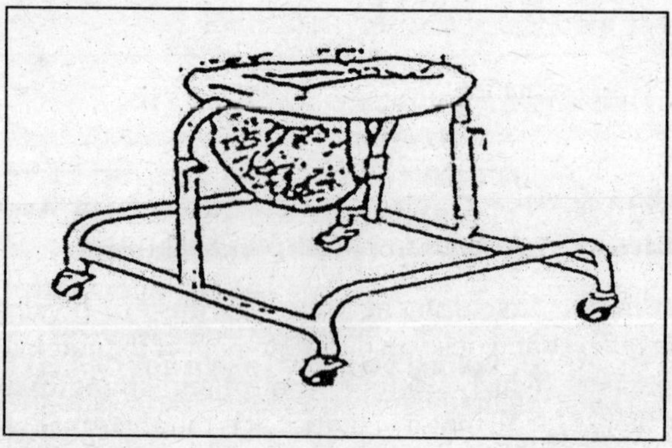

Instructional Activities

The following activities may be useful to the trainer for giving training to the children for using of Walkers.

1. Place a rattle or a toy of the child's choice on a chair in the corner of a room. Tell/gesture the child who is using an infant walker to move across the room and retrieve the toy. Then ask him to bring it to you.
2. Tell / gesture the child in an upright walker to follow a group of cardboard arrows that have been placed on the floor.
3. Play a "retrieval" game. Tell the child to move forward in the walker to retrieve a toy or object from a chair.

Use of Crutches

Crutches are used to increase balance and stability as well as to reduce or eliminate stress on weight bearing joints. Basically they compensate for loss of muscle control. However, any assistive device should be used only after the appropriate medical consultations.

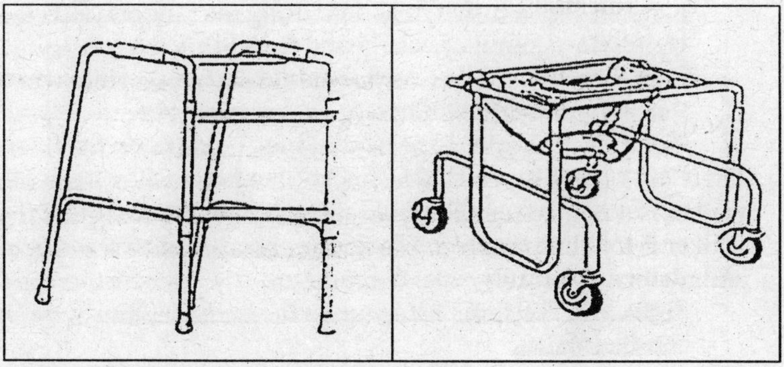

Instructional Activities

The following activities may be useful to the trainer for giving training to the children for using of crutches.

1. Show the child the four-point gait. This gait offers maximum support because there are always three points of contact with the ground. The cycle for the child to follow is (1) right crutch forward, (2) left foot forward, (3) left crutch forward and (4) right foot forward. Assist the child in practising this gait pattern.
2. When appropriate, tell the child to practise going form one end of the room to the other using two-point gait. This requires the child to be able to balance on one leg and involves a significant amount of skill.
3. At home, take the child to a community event such has Holi celebrations or Diwali Mela. Assist him when necessary. Wait until he is ready and moves independently with crutches inside the house before you take him out.

Use of Canes

Canes provide less support than crutches. Some canes are weighted with lead to provide added stability but most are not. Canes are of various types e.g. wood, aluminum, tripod cane and so on.

Instructional Activities

The following activities may be useful to the trainer for giving training to the children for using of canes.

1. Indicate to the child that he should walk towards you using

his cane. Indicate that he should bring the cane and affected leg forward simultaneously and then bring the unaffected limb forward. Practise with the child and correct him when this sequence is not followed.

2. Place empty paper cups next to the 'x' marks on the floor. Plan a game in which the children walk to each 'x' and pick up the empty cup. The child with the maximum cups at the end of a time limit wins the game and should be rewarded.
3. In the community, take the child to a street where there is a high curb. Tell him to step up on the curb the same way he climbed stairs.

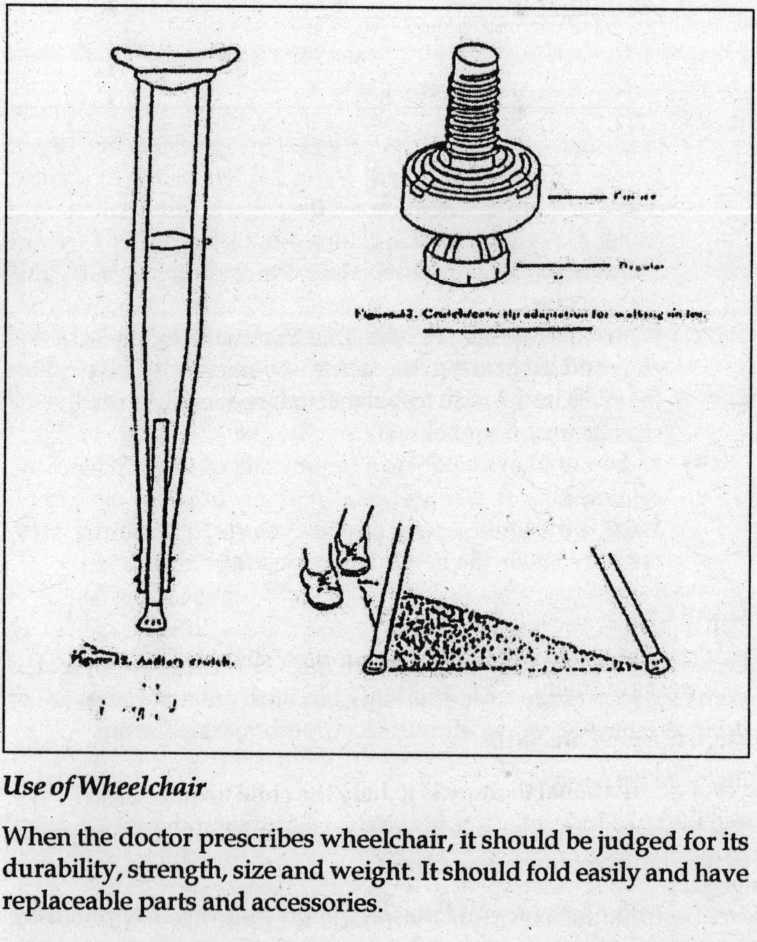

Use of Wheelchair

When the doctor prescribes wheelchair, it should be judged for its durability, strength, size and weight. It should fold easily and have replaceable parts and accessories.

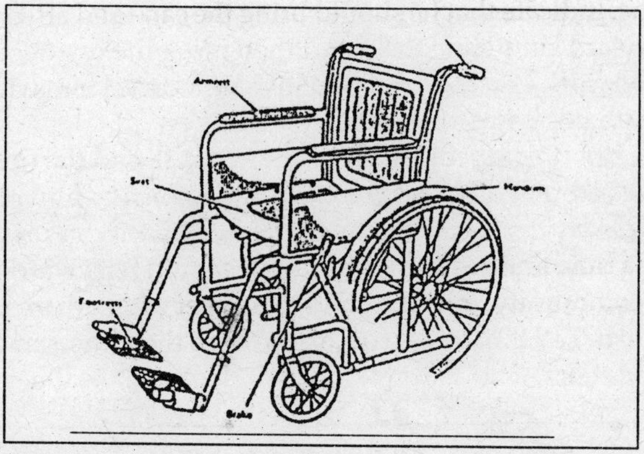

Instruction Activities

The following activities may be useful to the trainer for giving training to the children for using of crutches.

1. First practise by yourself how to unfold and fold a wheelchair. Show the child how to unfold a folded wheelchair.
2. Show the child to close the wheelchair. First check to see if the arms are locked. Fold up the footrests. Make a fold in the seat from above or below. If above, pull up, closing the chair. Assist the child in carrying out each of the steps.
3. Show the child how to use his wheelchair seat belt.
4. Ask the child in a wheelchair to wheel the chair a very short distance. Show the child how to lock and unlock the brakes of an empty chair.
5. Stand behind the child and call him to come to you in a backward movement. Show the child how to make/ turns in his wheelchair. Also show how if the child is in bed, can be transferred to wheelchair. Supervise all the actions till the child is independent. Use various prompts suitably and fade support gradually.

Acquisition of Self-Care Skills

The focus of occupational therapy is to help the child acquire basis self-care skills by reducing the motor problems. Attention should be particularly directed to feeding, toileting, bathing, brushing and dressing skills. The acquisition of eating skills is very complicated in children with motor problems. Emphasis is placed on proper body positioning. Eating utensils are sometimes modified as seen in Figure below:

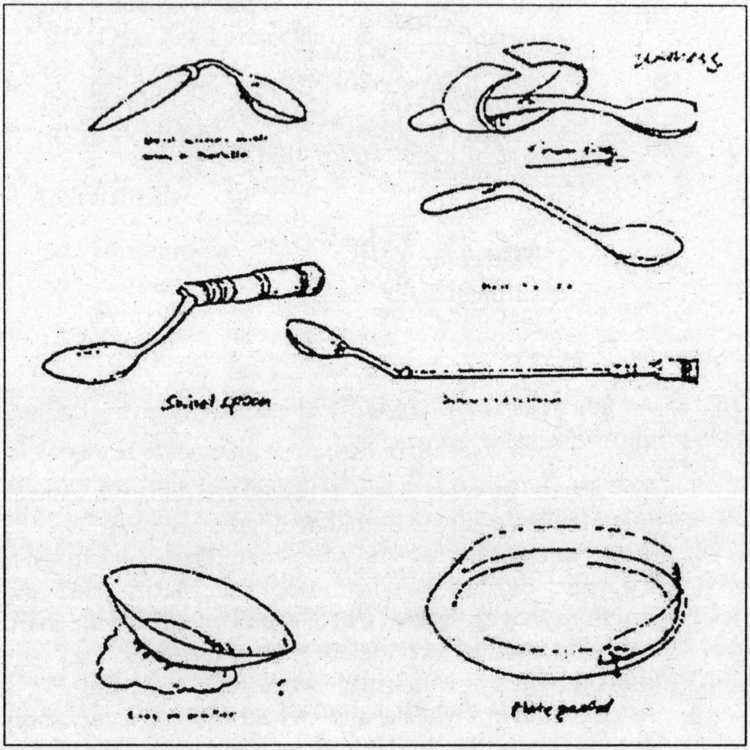

Feeding

Feeding is a major problem with children with mental retardation. There may be difficulties in one or more areas.

1. Oral Problem

- String biting reflex
- Tongue thrust
- High arch palate
- Difficulty in biting and chewing ability
- Difficulty in swallowing
- Persistence of sucking reflex etc.
- Dental problem

Remedial Methods

- Press the tip of the tongue with spoon.
- Keep the food a little deeper into the mouth. Otherwise the food will be stuck to the plate.
- Keep boiled carrot or potato in between the teeth. Model by biting them or pressing in jaw area to close the mouth.
- Wash the mouth thoroughly after eating.

2. Postural Difficulties

- Lack of head control
- Lack of sitting balance
- Lack of ability to maintain a straight position.

Remedial Methods

Use adapted materials like a chair with backrest or low cut-out table depending on the ability of the child.

1. Hand to Mouth Coordination Problem

- Unwanted movement of head and hand
- Lack of ability to grasp and release
- Lack of coordination.

Remedial Methods

Use adapted spoon, plate and glass to suit the needs of the children

> Would you like to knowhow Manish who is 2.5 years old and spastic, (CP) was helped to feed himself?
>
> Manish was functioning at 6 months level. He was initially unable even to finger – feed himself. He could not bring his hands to midline without assistance and he could only attempt to pick up small bites of food in raking motion. In order to help Manish, adaptation were made. A high chair was modified to inhibit extension reflexes and to facilitate normal eating movements. Over a period of three months Manish learn to pick up food placed on the table at midline and bring it to mouth in 10 seconds.

Adaptations in Bathroom and Toilet

The following points may be useful to the trainer for giving training to the children for adaptations in bathroom and toilet:

- Use modified mugs with thicker handles to make it easier for the child to hold.
- Handle bars in the bathrooms help the child to hold and balance self.
- For severely retarded children use big tubs for sitting and strap him to the pipe so that he/she can balance him/herself. Take care that it does not hurt him.
- In toilets, handrails and adapted toilet seats or a rope suspended form the ceiling can help maintain balance in sitting/squatting position.
- A hosepipe fitted to the tap will help in supply of water to the body part to be washed after toileting.

Dressing

Dressing is one of the important skills, which leads the child towards independence. As far as possible, the child should be taught to dress independently. The following points may be useful to the trainer for giving training to the children for dressing:

- Use of loose garments is necessary for easy handing.
- Neck should be bigger for the child to pull it easily.
- Adaptations like, Velcro, elastic or zip will be useful instead of buttons.
- Teach the spatial concepts while teaching dressing skills.
- Children with severe motor problems can be taught dressing in lying position also be turning him to the sides.
- Child who has sitting ability can be made to sit on a stool and train him in pulling the pants up.
- Handlebars or such support to the walls help the child in holding with one hand and pushing the dress up with the other.

General Instructional Activities

Various general activities are listed below. Teacher may select the appropriate activity keeping in view the age and level of the child. Help can be provided as and when necessary:

1. Gross Motor Activities

The following points of gross motor activities may be useful to the teacher for giving training to the children with retardation:

- Have children participate in various styles of jumping i.e. pair jumping in which one child faces another and hold hands and then jump together to the count of 10 or line jumping, rabbit jumping and so on.
- Have children participate in various types of creeping activities e.g. turtle crawl, snake crawl, or creeping through a course made of boxes or chairs.
- Have children take water in a container up to the brim and ask them to pick up the container and bring it to same specified point. This will help in walking with acceptable posture.
- Let children walk through a maze designed by the teacher.
- Lay the wooden ladder flat on the ground and have the children step into each square between the rungs.
- Have the children walk on the balance beams.
- Have the children participate in various types of walk e.g. barefoot walk, walking on a line, walking sideways. A game can be played where children will walk like duck, dog and so on.
- Have the children participate in various types of hopping activities like hop on their left foot, hop on their right foot, hop as quietly as they can or as low as they can.
- Have the children participate in various types of rolling activities like ball roll, towel roll and so on.
- Have children bounce the ball on the target which could be large in the beginning about 3 square. Have children see how often they can hit the target and have their partner catch the ball.
- To develop running abilities, have children participate in relay race.
- Have children play team sports as *kho-kho*, basketball, football or chain.
- Play a game in which you place cards (with pictures) around the room (like 4 toe touches, 3 push-ups, 10 jumps, 5 bent knee sit ups, etc.), have children go to each card and perform the activity.
- Use drama for body awareness and control of movement. Blindfold children and have they pretended that they are made of a substance that melts in the sun i.e., snow men, ice cream canes and so on.

- Here are recreational activities for gross motor skill development e.g. camping, hiking, etc.
- To assist children requiring more attention to motor activities, peer tutors can be used. Those peers provide one-on-one attention, praise and assistance. Let them work under the teacher supervision.

2. Fine Motor Activities

The following points of fine motor activities may be useful to the teacher for giving training to the children with mental retardation:

- A teacher may slowly move a straw and the child (who is being trained) should be asked to put toothpick inside.
- Here the child plays with balls using, initially large plastic balls, later large play ground balls then smaller balls.
- Let the child place small objects into a bowl and then fish them out with in a specific time.
- Have the child ring hand bells, turn doorknobs and unlock with keys.
- Allow the child to do activities with fingers e.g., squeezing tiny sponge, squeezing cardboard, spreading rubber band wide with straight fingers.
- Let the child participate in paper folding.
- Have the child practice block building, pegboard and copying models.
- Collect pairs of buttons that feel different from each other. Have children match up the pairs.
- Play a game where clothes are put in three piles e.g. put the piles in three different places. Have the children walk, jump or skip to each pile, find a garment and put.
- Provide exercise where the children will be helped to screw the nuts on the bolt till it is tight. Make sure that nuts and bolts join two pieces of some object.
- Place small objects in the tub with the sand and have the children retrieve the objects using different tools like tongs, spoon, or spatula.
- Introduce cutting tasks where the child will use scissors.
- Encourage children to make the game board, which they can use to play. For example, children can make a game

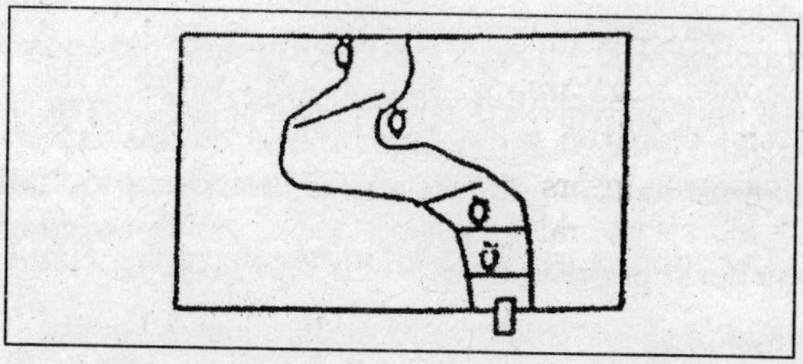

board sticking the string or toothpicks to the board in a ladder form. Play with a counter.

- Involve the children in interesting small motor activities. Fabric pieces about 2″ long and 1″ broad could be taken. Put a small button on one end and a buttonhole on the other. Let the children button the material together in a sequence to make a lace or something such pattern.
- Games can be played in which children match another set of objects already on string and children string in the same pattern or string by command.
- Finger painting can be had in making greeting cards and later, painting with large brushes can be encouraged.
- Encourage playing dot games. Construct a sheet with dots only and let children make their own drawing by joining dots.
- For older children constructing model planes and cars can enhance fine motor skills.
- Craft activities like airplanes; folder fans and purse can be encouraged.
- Pottery and clay activities can help improve fine motor coordination.
- Decoration on display board with paper cut patterns; cutting paper and stapling handouts are the other activities that can be encouraged.

Children with Mental Retardation with Motor Problems in General Classroom

Assess the ability of the student, the trainer may observe how he performs; consult the parents, teacher and others involved in the students education for suggestions in giving the adaptation. Adaptations should be in the following way:

1. It should allow access to the task.
2. The teacher should know how to use adaptations.
3. It should not restrict the movement of normal person.

Writing Adaptations

The following points may be useful for writing adaptations:

1. A pad of sheets (paper) rather than loose sheets.
2. Use of masking tape or a clipboard.
3. Use of control board.
4. Rubber strip on the back of a pad, use of magnetic board on iron desk to prevent slipping.
5. Velcro to attach items to a desk or wheelchair or lap tray.
6. Use of pens and pencils that require less pressure.
7. A rubber band around the shaft of the pen, a small ball over the writing instrument.
8. Use of typing aids such as a pointer stick to a head.
9. A line spacer that holds written materials while typing.
10. Computer assisted programme for functional academics.
11. Audio student assignments. (Can be operated with a single switch).
12. Allow student to write single letter or a one-word response.
13. Worksheets and tests that direct students to put lines through correct answers.
14. Computer can be equipped with variety of switches that allow students to operate single movement.
15. Alternate keyboards offer several features such as providing a large letter by pad over them, standard key boards, removing the need for simultaneous key provision.
16. Touch sensitive screens also to enable to respond to instructions and questions by touching specific areas of the screen.
17. Oral responses—speech synthesizers voice the responses that students with severe speech impairment type on the computer.
18. Communication boards allow the students to indicate their response.

Adaptations During Reading

The following points may be useful during reading adaptations:

1. Book holders, reading stands that adjust to inclining, sitting and standing positions.
2. Talking books enable students who cannot hold books.
3. Photo albums with plastic coversheet/flash cards, work cards etc.
4. Peer group help cooperation and assistance to the special children to complete the tasks.

Guidelines for Teaching Motor Skills

From the discussion above, it is clear that there are some points, which are very important to keep in mind for the trainer while developing motor skills in children e.g.

1. Design an environment in such a way that facilitates movement. Provide abundant opportunity for movement. Activity area in the classroom should be so arranged to allow for easy movement. Encourage interactions at home and in the community.
2. Consider safety when structuring the home and school environment for movement.
3. Teach specific movement as a part of an activity. This practice not only facilitates acquisition of specific movement but also can facilitate acquisition of behaviour in other areas. E.g. in training the child for fine motor activity the child learns to button his clothes and hence get dressed, which is a self-help skill.
4. Provide variety of structured (teacher directed) and unstructured (child directed) opportunities for movement. Schedule time, each day for outdoor, gross motor and play activities.
5. Encourage independence and development of motor skills in young children with disability. Use adaptive equipment keeping in view the child's needs.
6. Select appropriate activity/material for developing find motor skills keeping in view the child's problem.
7. Skill selected for the training should be functional that is they should serve a useful purpose in child's life and improve control of environment. Behaviours such as proficient locomotion and head control are more functional than standing on one foot or jumping from high platform.

8. Ensure that maintenance and generalization of gross motor behaviour takes place. To accomplish this, teacher should work with parents in selecting skills to be developed and then expect reinforcing those skills in other situations.
9. Motor skills should be facilitated in a game format. It increases the likelihood of maintenance and generalization. It also promotes social interactions and opportunities for fun and recreation.

Meeting Educational Needs

The teacher and the peer group are the important supporters for the successful integration of a child with cerebral palsy and mental retardation. The teacher and the peers in the classroom can encourage the child in the classroom to meet the individual's needs. Here, following points are important:

- If the child is using a wheelchair the desk or tray should be provided at such a height so as to enable the child to reach it without experiencing any discomfort. All the materials should be within the reach of the child.
- If the child's hands are affected you may have to provide him with a thick handle pen or pencil. Other children can help the child by taking down notes for him. If the child has severe motor problem help for writing may be provided. It may be necessary during the examination:
  - Special writing materials may be needed if the hand, arm or joints are affected.
  - Appoint a friend or peer to carry or bring material to the student's desk.
  - Allow more time to work and allow him more time to complete each task.
  - Give homework that he can handle.
  - If one hand is affected, teach the child to use the other hand.
  - Make the peer group understand the condition of the child and help when needed.
  - Encourage the peer group to push the wheelchair gently to prevent any possible injury.
  - Educate the peer group by explaining that the child with mental retardation is like other children and should be treated like one among them.

❖ Persuade the peer group not to tease the child for being different.

Positioning the Child in Class

For the positioning of the student the following points are important:

1. The head should be straight; the body symmetric, the arms straight, both hands in use and weight bearing should be equally distributed.
2. Functional position should be comfortable.
3. Seating adaptations for children (to meet specific needs) like special cushions, corner seats, wheelchairs, cut-out tables, and walkers should be provided.
4. Teachers should see that the aids do not restrict a child's movement.
5. Educational goals for individual students must be developed on the basis of evaluation data.
6. Consider the present physical and communication capabilities of the child.

School Responsibilities

To provide educational facilities for the child's development, the schools should do the following things:

1. Take the assistance of resource teacher's in dealing with children with special needs.
2. Evaluate the present and future needs of the child and programme according to the priority needs of the child.
3. Encourage parents in bringing up a child with mental retardation like any other citizen of the society.
4. Accept the child with mental retardation and encourage others to do the same.

Teacher's Role

After the parents it is the responsibility of the teacher to mould the child in a proper way. The teachers may play this role by doing the following things:

1. The Teacher has to be sensitive to the needs of the child.
2. Allow the child to learn at his own individualized pace.

Some Examples of Assistive Devices

The followings are some assistive devices for the children with associated disabilities.

Feeding and Drinking Aids

As the child becomes developmentally ready to feed himself, he may need some aids to make this possible. Adaptations of utensils are useful. Some of them are illustrated bellow:

Adapted Spoons

Adapted spoons are given in the following box. A regular spoon can also be adapted with foam or rubber tubing:

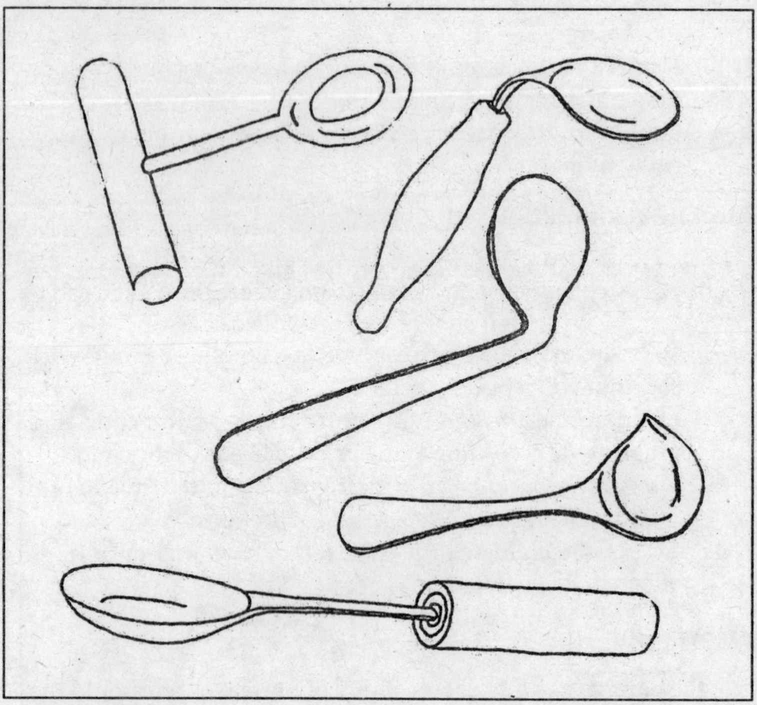

Tap Turner, Soap Mitt, Tooth Brush

Adapted Tap turners, Soap Mitt, Tooth brush shown in the following box may be used:

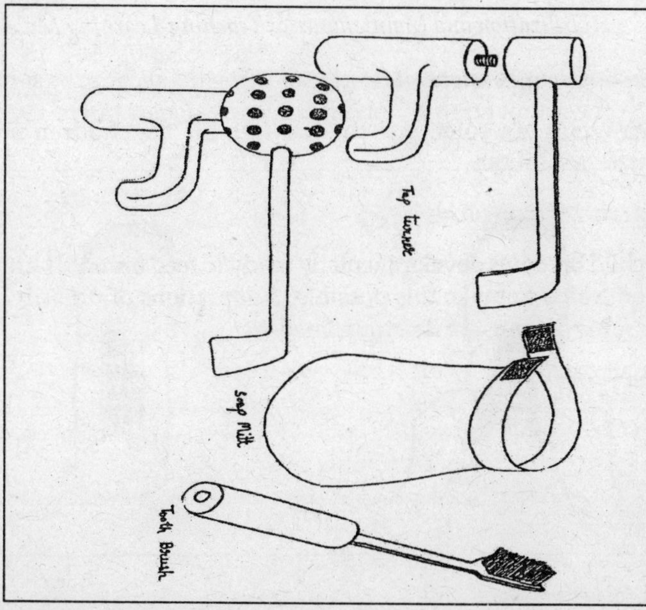

Velcro Fasteners

The Velcro tape has a great many use for easy to wear garments. There are no moving parts to the closure, the tape cannot sag and it opens at a touch. It grips two surfaces of nylon tape that adhere to each other securely yet open quickly and easily from either end. Velcro can be easily washed but should never be ironed with a hot iron.

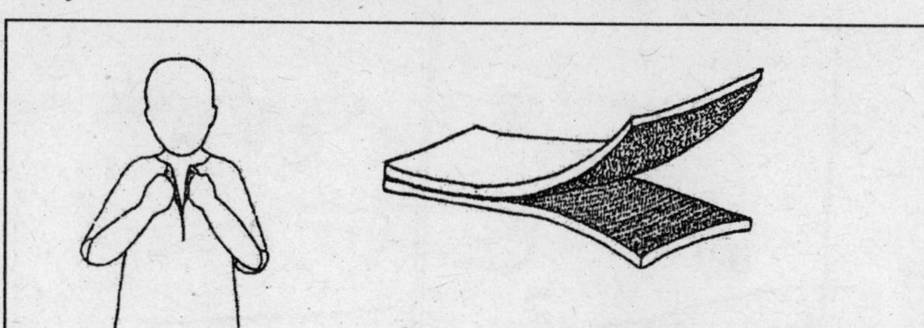

Shoe

Elastis shoelaces eliminate lacing by allowing the shoes to be slipped on and off without tying or untying. Velcro fasteners can be used on boots to eliminate shoelaces.

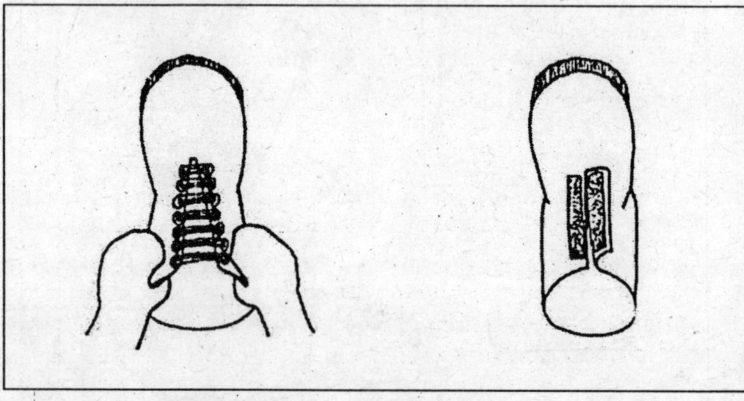

Magnetic Letters and Board

Letters of alphabet and numbers can be used on the board to learn to spell and count and then to communicate by building words.

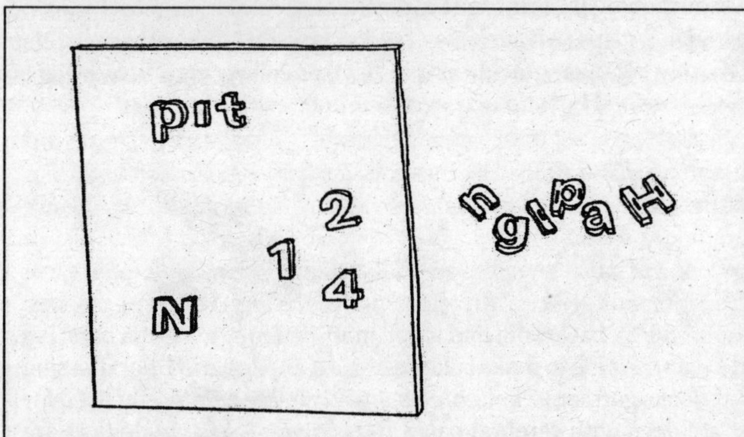

Large Pencils, Adapted Pencils, Adapted Paint Brush

Adapted pencils and paint brush as shown in the following box may be used:

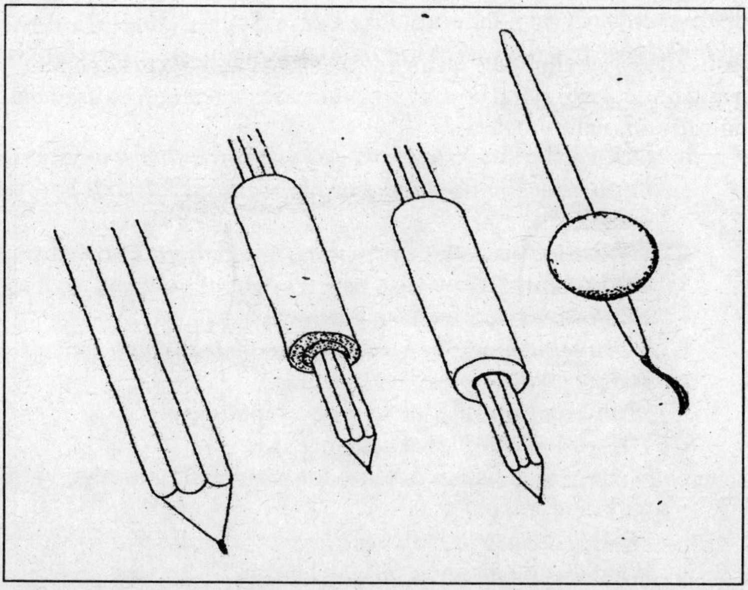

Unit Summary

Assistive/adaptive devices are specially designed devices to help children with associate disabilities in their independently functioning as possible. They may become mobile with the help of walker, crutches, cane and wheel chair from one place to another. Custom modifications in utensils are helpful to improve feeding skills. Such type of devices help them as remedial methods to sort out the difficulties faced by these children in one or more areas. For maintenance of posture to improve head control, sitting balance and ability to maintain a straight position, chair with backrest or low cut-out table are designed. To develop hand to mouth co-ordination adapted spoon, glass and plates are designed devices. Adaptation in bathroom and toilet, modified mugs, handle bars, big tubs with the pipe to make balance himself are designed. For dressing skills loose garments, velcro, elastic and zip are commonly used for the children with cerebral palsy and autism. Assistive devices are suggested in this unit to improve the gross motor, fine motor, writing and reading skills. To meet the educational needs of a child with cerebral palsy and mental retardation, the teacher and the peer group are the most important supporters for the successful integration. Teacher/special educator plays the great role in coordination with parents to mould their children in proper way so that these can learn at his/her own individualized pace. Some examples are also given of assistive devices in this unit to improve various activities.

Check Your Progress

1. Discuss the importance of adaptive and assistive devices in improving the learning process of the child with special needs.
2. What do you mean by writing adaptations and reading adaptations? How can you use effectively the writing adaptations and reading adaptations?
3. Write some guidelines for teaching motor skills.
4. Write two examples of eating aids.
5. Write two examples of writing adaptations.
6. Write two examples of dressing aids.
7. Write two assistive devices for a mentally retarded child with cerebral palsy.
8. What is the use of crutches?
9. What do you mean by talking books?
10. Name two major problems with mentally retarded children in feeding.
11. Write the remedial methods in postural difficulties.

Assignment/Activities

Identify a mentally retarded child with cerebral palsy and design a systematic individualized Educational Programme in each of self-care skills and prepare adaptive/assistive devices for developing each skill.

Point for Discussion/Clarification

After going through the Unit trainees may like to have further discussion on some points and clarification on other. They may note down these points for further discussion.

UNIT–4

STRUCTURE

- Types, Selection and Utility of TLM Points to be Considered : Using Natural Environment as TLM
- Various Types of TLM
- Various Multi-Sensory Teaching-Learning Materials
- Application of Computer in Teaching-Learning Process
- Selection of Teaching Materials and Aids
- Utility of TLM
- Multipurpose Utility of Learning Aids
- Low Cost Aids
- Points to be Considered for Using Teaching Aids
- Unit Summary
- Check Your Progress
- Assignment/Activities
- Point for Discussion/Clarification

Unit–4

Types, Selection and Utility of TLM Points to be Considered in Using Natural Environment as TLM

We have seen in the preceding unit that the teaching aids and teaching materials (LTM) are very helpful in teaching-learning process, both for normal and children with mental retardation.

The utility of TLM in children with mental retardation is much higher because of their intellectual functioning is sub-average and may also be suffering from other disabilities, such as visual and hearing impairments and speech deficits. Therefore, special teachers must know the value of teaching materials and teaching aids for both individual and group teaching programmes for children with M.R. He should never fully rely on verbal teaching, as it is least effective with these children. Therefore, a good special educator uses less verbal methods, but more methods of teaching and learning for children with M.R. He should also use visual aids and provide practical learning experiences in real life situation.

Various Types of TLM

There are different types of teaching aids, which can be used by the special teachers in classrooms. Some of them are as under:

1. *Visual Aids*

- *(a)* Blackboard
- *(b)* Charts, pictures
- *(c)* Models
- *(d)* Motion pictures, film strips
- *(e)* Slides
- *(f)* Flannel graph
- *(g)* Bulletin board

2. *Audio-Visual Aids*

(*a*) Slide projector
(*b*) Magic lantern
(*c*) Over head projector
(*d*) Epidiascope
(*e*) Film projector
(*f*) Gramophone
(*g*) Radio
(*h*) Tape recorder
(*i*) Television
(*j*) Video cassette recorder/ player

3. *Activity Aids*

(*a*) Museum
(*b*) Aquarium
(*c*) Garden
(*d*) Kitchen
(*e*) Workshop
(*f*) Laboratory
(*g*) Fairs
(*h*) Exhibitions

Various Multi-Sensory Teaching-Learning Materials

Teachers at present have, at their disposal, a wide variety of multi-sensory teaching-learning materials. For each multi-sensory material to be used, hardware and software are the essential requirements. The 'term software' is used to describe tangible stimulus items, whereas 'hardware' designates equipments and related electronic and mechanical components. A tape-slide (hardware) is used to produce audio as well as visual parts of a teaching unit. The recorded programme on the tape and slide is software. Some of the important Multi-sensory teaching-learning materials are:

(*a*) Tape-slide
(*b*) Video-tapes
(*c*) Educational Television (ETV)
(*d*) Closed Circuit Television (CCTV)
(*e*) Motion Picture
(*f*) Teaching Machines
(*g*) Computer/Information Technology
(*h*) Tele-conferencing

Each of the multi-sensory material used in teaching learning is explained in detail in the following paragraphs:

Tape-Slide

It is a kind of multi-sensory teaching-learning material wherein the audio tape is synchronized with the slides, thus provides audio as well as visual both learning experiences to the learner. In this system, synchronized audio and slide (tape-slide) presentation involve the use of a slide projector which is linked to a specially coded-audio tape, the tape both presenting audio tape, the tape both presenting audio information and controlling the automatic changing of slides. A computer can also be used to control sophisticated multi projector audio-visual presentation. merits and demerits of tape-slides are given below:

Merits of Tape-slide

- Tape-slides can be used for mass instruction and groups.
- It is relatively easy and simple to use.
- High quality full colour slides can have a greater impact than video.

Demerits of Tape-slide

- If one is using a projector, a darkroom would be needed.
- It is difficult for the learners to take notes because of darkroom.
- It requires suitable equipment, including a synchronization unit, to link the projector and an audiotape.
- It is bit difficult to set as compared to the Video and TV.

Video-Tapes

Video advances in electronics have resulted in the development of black and white and colour videos—since the sixties. Video-tapes have emerged as a powerful teaching-learning tool. This has great possibilities in the classroom. Not only can the programme be played at the proper moment decided by the teacher but it can be stopped mid-way through and re-started and sections of the material can be replayed, if required.

Merits of Video-Tapes

- It is a versatile teaching-learning aid.
- It is less expensive to produce and exhibit.
- It is re-recordable.
- It is excellent for displaying movements.
- It can bring a wide range of concrete examples.
- It is particularly useful to stimulate interest, provide an overview and present material for discussion.
- It is possible to capture the text, graphics and computer

animation and computer processed images in a video programme.
- It can also act as a manifestation medium to display small objects, processes and microscopic work.
- It can be combined with computer. Interactive video opens a wide range of utility.

Limitations of Video Tapes

- It provides passive learning activity.
- It requires darkroom facility.

Educational Television (ETV)

Till recently television was basically regarded as a medium of entertainment. But now a day, the potential of television has been explored as an educational medium. Television can transmit a wide range of audio-visual materials including still pictures, objects and specimen. Television can provide an interesting and exciting change and also furnish variety in the learning situation.

Merits of Educational Television

Advantages of educational television could be as follows:

- Television can bring models of excellence to the viewers. One can see and listen to a scientist, creative teacher, great poet and many more specialists in person.
- Television can find models of excellence to the teachers, especially in those fields where specialized teacher talent may be missing.
- Television can bring a world of reality to the classroom either through live presentation/broadcast or as mediated through film or videotape.
- Television provides an opportunity to the students to see and hear for themselves.
- Television can save the time of the teacher and the students.
- Television can overcome some of the barriers in teaching such as time, space, distance, invisible things and abstract ideas.
- Television lessons, once recorded on tape can be repeated any number of times.

Thus, we can see that television is a very powerful medium of instruction and if properly integrated in classroom teaching, it can make teaching-learning process more effective, meaningful and interesting. In the words of Chu, G.C. and Schramm, (1967), "The effectiveness of television has now been demonstrated in well over 100 experiments and several hundred separate comparisons, performed in many parts of the world, in developing as well as industrialized countries, at every level from pre-school through adult, and with a great variety of subject-matter and method."

Limitations of Educational Television

However, educational television, despite having its own advantages, is also not free from limitations. Some of these limitations are:

- Educational television presentations are one directional. There is no scope for interaction.
- Students are not engaged in the teaching-learning activities. They are the passive listeners only.
- It is not a flexible media. Telecasting time is fixed.
- There is a limited role of students in deciding about the content of the telecast.

To get rid of some of the limitations of television, Video-disc and Video-tape records can be used to store television programmes and can be viewed as and when required. In our country Inter-University Consortium for Educational Communication, New Delhi is assisting Doordarshan in selecting and arranging to televise enrichment type of programmes. A time slot for the morning and afternoon telecasts are fixed for this purpose. These programmes are broadcasted in all subjects such as science, economics, art, agriculture, engineering, medicine and law. The clientele is also varied nature ranging from elementary level students to graduate students and also members of the community.

Recently the Indira Gandhi National Open University (IGNOU), New Delhi, in cooperation with Ministry of Human Resource Development has also launched an educational channel, known as 'Gyan Darshan'. This telecast is done with the help of satellite channel.

Closed Circuit Television (CCTV)

Closed Circuit Television (CCTV) is also being used increasingly as educational media. The use of closed circuit television system increases the size of the audience by allowing one teacher to address several classrooms or even schools and colleges at a time located at different places. The creative applications and use of the television camera can also produce a better presentation, such as the use of the close-ups, which can focus the audience's attention on a particular issue.

In this system the television programmes are produced in one studio room of the institution and can be viewed by the receiver placed in other classrooms but connected by cable to the coupler in the production room. A simple closed circuit television system is given below:

Simple Closed Circuit System

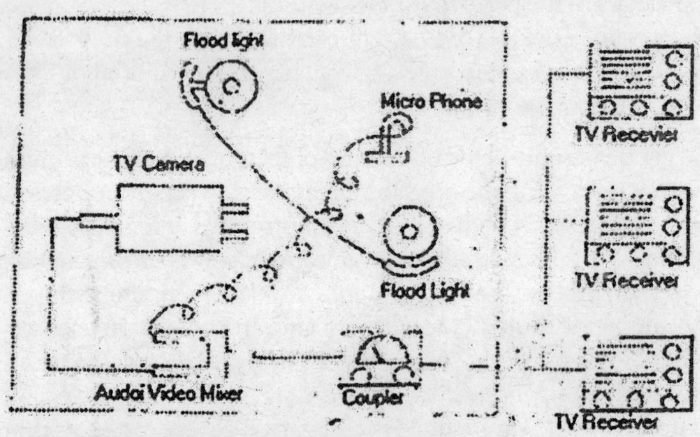

Merits of Closed Circuit Television (CCTV)

The CCTV has the Following Advantages:

- Through CCTV, one teacher can teach more than one section at a time.
- Through a two-way audio system, it can be made as inter-active.

- Through the use of CCTV, a lecture by an eminent person can be delivered to a large audience sitting at different places/locations.
- CCTV is very helpful in the demonstration of a lesson on motor skills to a large group of students.

Since a large number of educational video programmes are available on commercial basis, the closed circuit television can be used in schools to show video programmes to a large number of students in their classrooms at any specified time.

Motion Pictures

Motion pictures are extremely effective as multi-sensory teaching-learning material because it involves both audio and visual effects. The motion picture has got a variety of information, which is delivered over a short interval of time. This results in immediate and permanent retention of information in the minds of the students.

In a sound motion picture, sound is recorded and is reproduced along with the motion of the picture. Sound motion films have perforations on one side and sound track on the other side. Motion films are usually available in different widths. Usually 70 mm and 35 mm films are used for entertainment and require a large screen-at long distance 16 mm and 8 mm films are used for educational purposes. These films require smaller projector screen. Eight mm films are available in cassettes and are provided with magnetic sound track, while 70 mm, 35 mm and 16 mm films have optical sound track.

Merits of Motion Pictures

Motion pictures are very useful in the teaching-learning process. These are particularly useful in the following ways:

- These can be very helpful in showing certain skills or operations.
- Processes or events, which occur or occurred in distant places, can be brought to the classrooms.
- These can show the events and places of historical significance.
- These can be very useful in showing, in a short time, the

sequence of events or processes, which normally occur over a long span of time.
- It is possible to show processes, which cannot be seen with the naked eyes.

Teaching Machines

Educational technology movement began with the invention of teaching machines. A teaching machine is hardware for giving appropriate instructions to a student without the presence of a human teacher. It may range from a simple Manual or Mechanical device. A teaching machine performs the following functions:

- Displays an information.
- Ask student response.
- Evaluate, reinforces and controls for the nest display.

Sidney Pressey devised one of the very fast teaching machines with two wooden boards' answers board and keyboard with holes drilled in them. Students were provided with two Boards-Answer Board on the top and Key Board at the bottom with a plain paper sandwiched between them. While working with a teaching machine, a student introduces his pencil or pen through an appropriate hole in the answer board. If response were correct, pencil would go through in the Key Board making a hole in the plain paper. If the response is wrong, the pencil will leave a dot on the plain paper. The student should do it again till the correct answer or the pencil goes through in the Key Board Digging of a plain paper at the location of key holes correspond to the correct answer. This machine permits students to learn at their own pace and time. It is possible that a student may be allowed only once to respond.

Computer/Information Communication Technology

The most striking innovation in the field of educational technology is the use of computers in education, particularly for teaching and learning process. It has come to stay for long because of the following reasons:

- High data storage capacity
- High speed of operations
- Networking advantage
- Good interactivity with other devices and human beings

- Logical sequencing and control
- Easy portability
- Facilitation to individuality
- Consistency and accuracy

Tele-Conferencing

Tele-conferencing is a recent developed mode of interacting with others sitting at a distant place by circumventing costs of travel as well as time. As far as its educational application is concerned, it is a means to communicate and discuss educational issues and problems with groups of learners at different campuses and in different academic institutions. Tele-conferencing is also helpful in organizing teaching training programmes, seminars and conferences without incurring expending on travel costs for the delegates and teachers. It is a mode of interaction between two or more persons at long distance. There may be three different type of tele-conferencing system as follows:

- *Video Conferencing:* Face-to-face communication using Television and audio system.
- *Audio Conferencing:* Natural Extension of the person-to-person telephone calls to extent to more than 2 persons.
- *Computer Conferencing*: Text and graphics communication to participants who may access the control computer through type write terminals.

Keeping in mind the possibilities of different transmission, there can be a different configuration of tale-conferencing system.

(a) One-way transmission of electronic signals—Simplex.
(b) Two-way transmission of electronic signals—Duplex.
(c) One-way at a time in either direction—Half-Duplex.

Video conferencing requires duplex transmission to permit two-way movement of audio and video signals.

Merits of Tele-Conferencing

Some of the advantage of tele-conferencing is listed below:

- It provides a good support to student residing at far off place.
- It saves travel and other costs.

- It is easy to schedule group discussion and conferencing by telephones.
- It helps in providing immediate feedback and also quick remedial actions, incase of need.
- It makes available experts of the area who are otherwise busy.
- Computer conferencing is adaptable for use by challenged person.

Limitations of Tele-Conferencing

The tele-conferencing mode has also certain limitations:

- Video conferencing has high cost of installation and operation.
- Video conferencing requires number of electronic devices.
- Video conferencing requires high level of expertise.

Application of Computer in Teaching–Learning Process

Computers are being increasingly used for classroom instruction as also for individualized and distance education. Application of computer in teaching-learning process is known as Computer Based Instruction (CBI) or Computer Aided Learning (CAL) in U.K and Computer Assisted Instruction (CAI) in the USA. All these names refer to on-line direct interactive learning through the computer. It can be organized in various instructional modes like:

1. *Tutorial Mode:* Where information is presented to the learner in small bits followed by a question for self-check. The student's response to the question is analyzed and feedback is given.

2. *Drill and Practice Mode:* Where learner is presented with a number of graded examples on various concepts, facts and principles, which are learnt earlier. All the correct responses given by the learner are reinforced and wrong ones diagnosed and remedial measures provided.

3. *Simulation Mode:* Where learner is presented with simulated situations very close to the real ones for learning. Simulations are done where risk factors are very high. For example, simulation of an aero-plane in flight or a nuclear reaction etc.

4. *Discovery Mode:* Where learner is encouraged to learn through trial and error approach to arrive at correct solution of a complex problem.

5. *Gaming Mode:* Where learner is encouraged to learn games. The extent of learning depends upon the type of a game. Games on spellings and general knowledge are two examples.

Merits of CAI/CAL/CBI

Advantages of CAI/CAL/CBI are given as under:

- It allows each student to work at his own pace, time and place.
- It provides immediate feedback and also remedial measure, if required.
- Information is presented in small bits, which enhances learning.
- It provides reinforcement of learning.
- It is interactive, students can ask questions also.
- The graphic facility available with computer. It further enhances its capability of explanation.
- It is student-centered. It requires very less interference of the teacher.
- Now-a-day CAI/CAL/CBI is commercially available which enhances its accessibility.

Selection of Teaching Materials and Aids

Special teachers have to select the materials carefully for their classes, keeping in mind the following principles. The materials should be

1. age appropriate, lower the age, simpler the aid and vice versa.
2. suited to the level of learners—their IQ, achievement and aptitude.
3. motivate children with mental retardation in learning individually or in groups.
4. readily available or easily improvised by teacher.
5. prepared from local resources and inexpensive.
6. accurate in representation of facts e.g., model or picture of rose must look like rose flower.

7. attractive, symmetrical and colourful for children.
8. related to the curriculum or the deficit skills of children selected by teacher for training.
9. prepared in easy and simple language, so that children can understand the concepts.
10. easy enough to make complex and difficult concepts, as simple and easy topic for children.
11. easy in manipulation in class.
12. neither too small nor too big for children to comprehend the message.
13. well-designed by artists by artists or teachers, as the case may be.
14. inspire children for further self-study in life ahead.

Utility of TLM

Anything taught in the classroom or a training situation need to be generalized for a child with retardation so that he applies the skill learnt to any appropriate situation. The teaching aids should be such that the child requires minimum assistance to learn and utilize the skill learnt. For instance, in the classroom a teacher would use abacus, sticks and such materials for teaching addition to children. Later the child learns to do addition on paper without using the aids. The next step should be to assess the child's ability to do addition in generalized situation. This can be done with simple materials. To quote an example, one can show to the child saying that father has bought 3 Rin soaps and 4 Liril soaps. How much soap has been bought? If such experiences are given along with teaching of addition, transfer of learning will be minimized. It should also be remembered that using certain materials as a learning aids might result in their becoming indispensable. Such learning aids must be avoided. For example, there are instances, where the children without physical disabilities who have been toilet trained only on a potty, refused to use an Indian type of water closet and tending to even remain constipated.

Multipurpose Utility of Learning Aids

Any aid bought or prepared for teaching should have a variety of use. The aid used for training in motor co-ordination can be used for teaching colours numbers, grouping, sorting, size texture and so on. Such aids include simple wooden beads of various sizes, building blocks nest of baskets and so on. But one should remember that such materials are more suitable as aids at pre-primary and primary level where younger children are trained. For older children age appropriate multipurpose materials should be used.

Low Cost Aids

Materials available in and around the home are the best aids to train children as they are constantly used. Children with mental retardation are generally found to be interested in music, simple musical instruments can be tying small bells in tape or belt, and rattles made using various sized stones in empty shampoo bottles.

Small children with delayed milestones, who need training to sit, can be helped using empty cartoons of television or such materials. Make the child sit inside the box in the corner, tie the box from outside so that it does not fall apart when the child in learning to sit. Give toy to the child to manipulate. Toys could be held in a string from end-to-end on the box if the child needs to be motivated for reaching for objects. Such small adaptations made in the existing materials will go a long way in learning various skills. Teachers and trainers with creative ideas can develop many such low cost aids. While buying teaching/learning aids one has to consider the cost the utility and durability of the material to be bought.

To put it in a nutshell, learning aids are essential for training children in various skills, as multi sensorial input is one of the essential aspects of skill training. While selecting aids, one has to remember that the aids are, as far as possible utilized in day-to-day life, they are appropriate to the child who is being trained, durable and cost effective. In addition, the trainer should try his/her best to utilize the materials available in the home and community environment to teach the various skills to the child.

Points to be Considered for Using Teaching Aids

The individual differences in learning skills, retaining skills, and application of skill is very high in person with mental retardation. Hence, educator must select the most appropriate aids considering all the principle and factors to teach the children with mental retardation. Following points are important:

- While selecting the teaching aids various aspects had to be kept in mind. The purpose of the aids is a crucial aspect and it should have definite objective.

- Teaching proceeds from concrete to abstract; hence concrete objects and experiments are very crucial.
- Flexibility of use of aids for many different purposes and use of variety of aids to bring novelty in teaching-learning process is to be emphasized.
- Through knowledge of the content, the teacher must know the use and how to make the best use of the aids.
- While viewing, listening, reading the material; focus student's attention on specific things. The material must be arranged as per sequence of the lesson plan; this makes the presentation of the material easy.
- The effectiveness of the learning aids actually depends upon the achievement of the students; hence keep checking student's reaction.

Unit Summary

By going through the above unit we may conclude that there are various types of TLM and those TLM should be considered in teaching-learning process of the children with mental retardation, which has great utility in natural environment. Here, again the special educator plays an important role in selection of the need based, age based TLM which provide practical learning experience in the real life situations. Visual aids, audio-visual aids, activity aids, various multi-sensory teaching-learning materials are given in this unit to understand how to use them, what are their merits and demerits. The motion pictures are extremely effective multi-sensory teaching-learning material because it involves both audio and video effects. Special educators have to select the materials very carefully to meet the individualized needs of the child because anything taught in the classroom or in the training situation need to be generalized so that the child can apply them to any appropriate situations. All the learning aids should have the multipurpose utility in his/her real life. A special educator should have the skill to use effectively the low cost aids or used materials in teaching-learning process. Hence, he/she must select the most appropriate aids considering all the principles and factors to teach the children with mental retardation.

Check Your Progress

1. What are the different types of TLM available? Discuss the utility of them and the points to be considered while using them.
2. Explain various types of multi-sensory teaching-learning material. Also write their merits and demerits.
3. What are the role of charts, models and pictures in teaching a person with multiple disabilities?
4. Explain audio-visual aids.
5. Define communication board.
6. Explain CAI.
7. Write name of two mobility aids. Write name of two TLM for auditory stimulations.
8. Write name of two activity aids.
9. Write two principles of selection of teaching materials and aids.
10. What is multipurpose utility of learning aids?
11. Define Tele-Conferencing.

Assignment/Activities

Write the types of TLM commonly used in natural environment. What do you mean by motion pictures? How do you select and prepare the TLM for teaching cooking skills?

Point for Discussion/Clarification

After going through the unit trainees may like to have further discussion on some points and clarification on other. They may note down these points for further discussion.

UNIT–5

STRUCTURE

- Computer Assisted Instruction – Use of Available Educational Packages, Developing/Adapting Educational Software
- Developing Educational Software
- Learner/Computer Interaction
- Access and Current Trends
- Advantages of Computer Software
- Limitations of Computer Software
- Unit Summary
- Check Your Progress
- Assignment/Activities
- Point for Discussion/Clarification

Unit–5

Computer Assisted Instruction—Use of Available Educational Packages, Developing/Adapting Educational Software

Technology can play a powerful role at every step in a person's life, particularly in lives of those individuals who have special needs. Parents, teachers and service providers for students at every level want to know what options could expand the potential for their child or student to interact, learn and develop.

Computer Assisted Instruction has several types of instructional programmes namely, drill and practice, tutorial, educational games, demonstration, problem solving and discovery learning.

1. *Drill and Practice:* These softwares are developed to help the students practice the previously learnt materials on computer, thus enhancing automatic level of responding. Though it provides over learning, repetition and immediate feedback it may end up to be monotonous and have limited cognitive demands.

2. *Instructional Games:* They are highly motivating as learning occurs through games. It increases concentration, coordination and dexterity, but it has the threat of children wanting to play the games and not actually meeting the educational objectives.

3. *Simulation*: Experiences provided in simulations are analogous to real life situations, demanding active involvement of the student in problem solving. However, it

may be difficult to integrate this component in academic curriculum, which is structured and rigid.

4. *Tutorial:* This assists the child to work independently and provides for review of learnt materials. It has the facility to present instruction in sequential, step-by-step manner. Child's own motivation is a prerequisite for use of this software.

5. *Demonstration:* This allows the students and teachers to manipulate relationship among variables by pressing the keys and has presentation with colour, graphics and sounds that sustain interest.

6. *Problem-solving:* Computer as a tool to solve problems is used in many areas, especially, in calculations, where the student analyses the problem and writes executable programme to get desired results.

7. *Discovery Learning*: This can be integrated in games and simulations and it allows a child to learn by exploration and experiences.

Developing Educational Software

Although we have access to numerous educational software in the Indian market, they are basically targeted for the regular curriculum. Beside, there are various other factors responsible for the failure of these software, which includes the following:

1. Software not adaptive to various types of disabilities.
2. Software not designed to suit different degrees of functional abilities.
3. Inadequate provisions for user control.
4. Poor flexibility of programmes.
5. Inadequate sequencing of institutional events.
6. Inadequate research done.
7. Hastily introduced without adequate field testing.
8. Unimpressing graphic screens.
9. Poor interaction between programmers and educators.

Learner/Computer Interaction

While designing special instructional software, following principles need to be taken care of:

(a) Questions

- Ask frequent questions.
- Ask appropriate questions (well placed, clearly phrased, and meaningful).

(b) Responses

- Provide prompts on when to respond and how to respond.
- Use an appropriate single character response format: with and without<enter>.

(c) Evaluation and Feedback

- Correct responses – evaluate responses meaningfully.
- Incorrect responses – provide a variety of feedback: confirmational, corrective and motivational feedback.
- Unanticipated responses – provide the answer after 2-3 tries.

(d) Data

- Collect data for management or revision purpose.

(e) Ease of Operation

- Make instructive always available and clear.
- Handle incorrect learner responses without 'crashing'.

Learner Control

- Allow options and choices whenever appropriate.
- Allow pacing or screen erases control.
- Allow optional review of text.
- Allow graceful exits.

Sequencing of Instruction Events

- Specify the audience and purpose or goals for the software.
- Specify the general structure or given an overview of the total lesson and paths through it.
- Specify learning objectives for each component.
- Elaborate from simple structure to the more detailed facts.
- Use concept, example, non-example, practice sequences, etc.
- Direct the learner's attention to the major concepts or points by providing visual cues such as words of a different colour, boxes spatial separation or lists.

- Provide different opportunities for the fast or experienced learner vs. the slow or inexperienced learner (adaptive tutorials, for example).

Graphic Screen Design

- Prepare the layout so that it is pleasing and easy to read with no annoying features.
- Separate instructions from main text area *via* view ports so that the learner is cued to look at a certain general position of the screen.
- Use graphics appropriately (instructional purpose).

Access and Current Trends

The technology advance in general education as well as special education is of recent origin. A pilot project on computer literacy was launched in 1985 by Department of Education in a number of regular schools. Presently in a number of states regular schools education includes computer literacy as a part of curriculum (Dutta, 1986). Word processor programmes in Indian languages have been developed for wider reach out. Production of adapted peripherals and add-on devices with indigenous softwares are rapidly increasing to suit the need of the disabled individuals. The biomedical engineering departments of the colleges of technology collaborate with special education programmes for development of suitable materials for the disabled persons in India. Following are some of the devices developed in India. Indian Institute of Research and Information Services (IRIS, 1994), New Delhi, developed (1) Writing aid for persons with motor disabilities. (2) Communication aid to children with cerebral palsy called 'Swarlipi', where an electronic interface provides access to computer using touch, movement of head, eyeball, blow energy or tongue (Anand, 1994). (3) The Indian Institute of Science (IISc), Banglore has developed three gadgets for the visually impaired individuals to manipulate a computer. In addition, speech synthesizer, electronic Braille short-hand machine have also been developed (Nair, 1994). The National Institute for the Handicapped are also experimenting with technology for the disabled individuals.

Advantages of Computer Software

As we all know, computers have changed the entire lifestyle of people.

Those with disabilities are no exception. In the area of mental retardation, where individualized instruction is essential, the computer is a boon. It provides the individual learning time to student. After training the teacher may allow the child to use the computer on his own, and she can attend to other children. The interactive programmes play the role of the teacher too.

The child's self-esteem is boosted when he proudly say he uses computers. Going with the principle of normalization it provides access to retarded children. The suitably selected softwares help as drill and practice for the content already taught by the teacher. The studies done at NIMH through multi-centred data collection on use of CAI revealed that even severely retarded children benefit from the programme, the students attention span increases and distractibility reduces, the students do their routine duties well if promised of computer time thus serving as a good reinforcement.

Limitations of Computer Software

When we look at limitations, affordability stands out as a major problem. CAI seems out of reach for majority students. Indian softwares are minimum thus having limited access, especially so, for education of those with mental retardation. The NIMH has developed a few exclusive softwares and is in the process of developing more of mentally retarded persons. Multilingual characteristic of our country in another problem in quick reproduction and use of softwares.

Transfer of training from computer to daily living activities is difficult in mental retardation unless the teacher takes extra efforts. Moreover, the teacher herself needs training in use of computers.

Unit Summary

Today, due to the advancements in the field of special education, one of the current trends occurred in the rehabilitation of persons with disabilities is the use of Computer Assisted Instructions. The use of technology for retarded children enhancing CAI programmes. Although CAI have advantages as well as limitations, but it has several types of instructional programmes and create interest in children with mental retardation. It is also to be considered that all the special educators must be trained in use of computers.

Check Your Progress

1. What is new and latest technology used in treating children with mental retardation? Explain its advantages and limitations.
2. How the computer assisted instructions help in various types of instructional programmes? Write the types of instructional programmes where we can use CAI.
3. What is the use of technology in teaching children with special needs?
4. What are the factors responsible for failure of developing software's for the persons with disabilities?
5. What are the principles needs in designing special instructional software?
6. Expand CAI.
7. Use of software's (2 users) in teaching with special needs.
8. Name list of advantages of CAI.
9. Name list of limitations of CAI.
10. What do you mean by Graphics Screen Design?
11. Write the name of the two software designed by National Institute of Mentally Handicapped (NIMH) Secundrabad.
12. Write two devices developed by IRIS (1994), New Delhi.

Assignment/Activities

Collect any two software of your choice for teaching persons with mental retardation and implement them during training programme and evaluate the progress of two children. Also write the feedback and self-evaluation in using CAI.

Point for Discussion/Clarification

After going through the unit trainees may like to have further discussion on some points and clarification on other. They may note down these points for further discussion.

Bibliography

1. RCI, 1998, Catalogue of TLM for all Disabilities.

2. Hendrickson, J. and Gable, R. (1990), Errors in spelling. In R. Gable & J. Hendrickson (Eds Assessing students with special needs (pp. 78-88), New York: Longrha).

3. Langone, J. (1990), *Teaching Students with Mild and Moderate Learning Problems*, Bostd Allyn and Bacon.

4. Upkaran–A Manual of Aids for the Multiply Handicapped by Spastics Society of India.

5. Jackman, H.L. (1999), *Sing Me a Story: Tell Me a Song*. California: Crown Press, Inc.

6. NIMH (2002), *Software Packages for Children with Mental Retardation.*

7. B.Ed. Special Education (MR), *Distance Mode*, MP Bhoj University, Bhopal– SESM-02, Block 3, Unit–2.

8. B.Ed. Special Education (MR). *Distance Mode*, MP Bhoj University, Bhopal– SEPG-01, Block 3, Unit–6.